SEEDS OF LIFE

Jules Beaulac

Translated by
Barbara Green and Geraldine Antaya, s.p.

Éditions Paulines

Originally published as *Aimer... Vivre sa vie*
by Novalis, Ottawa, Canada

Phototypesetting: *Les Éditions Paulines*

Cover: *Antoine Pépin*

Photos: *Jules Beaulac and Antoine Pépin*

Imprimatur: *Msgr. Jean-Marie Fortier,* Archbishop
            Sherbrooke, January 25, 1986

ISBN 2-89039-981-8

Dépôt légal — 1ᵉʳ trimestre 1987
Bibliothèque nationale du Québec
National Library of Canada

© 1987 Éditions Paulines
        250, boul. St-François nord
        Sherbrooke, Qué., J1E 2B9

Contents

II
GOSPEL LIGHTS

III
PRAYERS

IV
REFLECTIONS

V
PEOPLE

''I am never alone.
He Who sent me
is always with me''.

Jn 8:29

Introduction

You undoubtedly know of some cool woods
and colorful gardens.

When strolling in them,
you walk at your ease
and speed,
and stop when you please.

You sit beneath an oak tree
to feel the coolness of its shade,
you smell the violets' sweet scent,
you admire the magnificent roses,
you pick and eat a fruit,
you listen to the birds' songs...
Sometimes,
you pick a flower
or make a nosegay.

I would like to see you read through this book
in much the same way
as you stroll through the woods.
Here, you will glean a text to your liking.
There, you will find a word
that will embellish your life,
brighten your day.

This book should not be read in one sitting:
You would be quickly saturated!

Appreciate it according
        to your likes,
        to your speed,
        to your needs.

May it help you to LOVE and to LIVE.

I
FACTS

Puddles

It had rained heavily that evening:
the road was full of puddles
that sparkled like sequins.
The sunlight shining on them
made them seem like the pearls
in a great necklace.

A painter had set up his easel
at the corner of the street,
and, already with his brushes, palette and skill,
had made a bright painting.

Two small children were playing,
looking at their own saucy faces,
in a large puddle
which reflected their smiles.

Another little urchin,
complete with rubber boots,
had fun running
from one puddle to the next.
A natural clown
who could make his own happiness
from nothing at all.

Another, with a stick,
was joining up the puddles
with a carefully built canal,
probably a budding engineer.

A little girl had picked some daisies,
and floated the petals on the water,
humming softly to herself.

It was beautiful.
Life felt good.
Everyone was happy
and the street was one great poem!

Suddenly, a car shot by,
driven by someone hurried and tense.
He crushed the daisies,
broke the engineer's canals,
spattered mud over the painting,
sent water into the small boy's boots
and just missed hitting one of the children
who had been jumping puddles.

The world became dull,
life became grey,
the people became sad,
and the street became a small hell!

In life, we make it shadow or light...
Which side do we choose most often?

I saw...

I saw people,
men and women,
young people and children
come together
    to hear the Word of God,
    to pray to their Lord,
    to tell of
        their faith,
        their hopes,
        their love...
and that touched my heart!...

I saw
a doctor, a brilliant specialist,
acknowledge himself a sinner
before his community
and
beg of God
to win him over to His Love...
and that warmed my heart!...

I saw
an architect, a well known professional,
give his surplus
to the poor
and pray to love God alone...
and that brought a question to my heart!...

I saw
a mother
ask forgiveness of God

17

for her harsh criticism during the day
and
pray for those she had judged...
and that brought joy to my heart!...

I saw
a workman with rough hands
offer to the Lord
the disputes in his working environment
and
pray that justice might prevail...
and that brought tears to my heart!...

I saw
a young girl, with sobs in her voice,
pray to God
for her boyfriend who had left her for another...
and that shook my heart!...

I saw
a humble priest
pray for the coming of the "new man" in himself
and for the "life" of his community...
and that gave light to my heart!...

Yes, I tell you,
I saw
    sinners, humble and believing,
    believers, sincere and hopeful,
    hopeful souls, fervent and loving,
    loving people, simple and strong.
I saw
    the strength of the Word received in faith,
    the power of prayer celebrated
      in brotherly fashion,
    the grandeur of forgiveness, given and accepted.

I saw
    peace of soul,
    a joyful heart,
    a tender look,
    light on faces!
Yes, I saw all that... and marvelled!
And through it all...
I saw You, Lord!
I prayed to You!
And I envied them a little!
How good, how delightful it is for all
to live together like brothers *(Ps 133:1)*.

Sing the words and tunes of the psalms and hymns
when you are together;
and go on singing and chanting
to the Lord in your hearts... *(Ep 5:19)*.

Thirst...

For many weeks, it had not rained.
The earth was parched, shrivelled, cracked...
The wells were dry, the flowers withered...
The animals gasped for breath!

For days,
he had walked in the desert sand,
in the dust brought by the wind...
His face, wrinkled, dry, leather-like,
was burned by the sun!
His eyes were red and staring!
His throat was raw!
His step was unsteady,
he lurched and reeled!

Lo and behold,
the rain had come,
      fresh,
      warm,
      gentle!
It slowly, deeply penetrated the earth,
giving life to everyone and everything!
O beneficial rain!

Suddenly,
a child was there
bringing a bowl of water
to the stranger!
      fresh water,
      pure water,
      crystal-clear water!

It cooled the burning throat.
It relieved the swollen face.
It restored life to the dull eye!
O beneficial water!

As a doe longs
for running streams,
so longs my soul
for You, my God *(Ps 42:2)*.

God, You are God,
I am seeking You,
my soul is thirsting for You,
my flesh is longing for You,
a land parched weary and waterless.
I long to gaze on You in the Sanctuary,
and to see Your power and glory *(Ps 63:2)*.

I stretch out my hands,
like thirsty ground I yearn for You *(Ps 143:6)*.

The Lord will give strength to your bones
and you shall be like a watered garden,
like a spring of water
whose waters never run dry *(Is 58:11)*.

Anyone who drinks the water that I shall give
will never be thirsty again:
the water that I shall give
will turn into a spring inside him,
welling up to eternal life *(Jn 4:14)*.

Henry's wild cherry tree
or know when to leave

Henry owns a magnificent maple grove:
three thousand trees.

The other day,
he invited me to his sap-house
with a few other families.
We drank the boiled down sap by the cupful
and licked the maple taffy off the spoon!
Then we ate the traditional Canadian sugaring off food:
    pork rind,
    eggs poached in maple syrup,
    ham…
and finished the meal with taffy on snow.
A real feast!

After dinner,
Henry said:
"Come make a round with us!"
The maple sap was running… one drop per second!
Off we went!

There were maple trees everywhere… naturally!
Pails everywhere… too!
Brimming over with sweet water!
At one turn of the forest path,
we suddenly found ourselves
before an odd scene:
there were maple trees, for sure,
but smaller than elsewhere,

and right in the midst of them
was a stately wild cherry tree,
lording over them all!

What a beautiful titan!
Its bark was almost white!
Its trunk so huge that my arms could not enfold it!
What a stately tree!
It was lord of the forest
superbly reigning over its surrounding subjects!

''You see this cherry tree,''
said Henry,
''it's taking up all the place,
the maple trees can't grow.
Its branches cut off the sunlight
and its roots take all the moisture in the soil.
I shall cut it down next winter!''
I spontaneously said:
''You're not going to cut down
   such a magnificent tree!''
Henry said:
''Here we make maple syrup,
not cherry syrup!
My maple trees must grow
and that cherry tree harms them.
It has gone on long enough.
Anyway it's only good for firewood.
See, that's life!''

* * *

23

"That's life!"

Among men,
there are always some who stand out:
    greater intelligence,
    greatness of works,
    profoundness of influence,
    power of intuitions...
The builders,
the leaders of communities, of nations,
tha natural leaders,
are ordinarily of this stamp.

So are
    rulers,
    dictators,
    tyrants... also!
They wield power,
not only in action,
but in thought,
even in affection!
Having given shade,
    coolness,
    strength,
to those around them,
they end up stifling them,
preventing growth
and blossoming out!
They end up being
    jealous,
    suspicious,
    touchy,
    grumpy,
    fussy!

They move
>from service to power,
>from sharing to possessiveness,
>from love to monopolisation,
>from authority to tyranny,
>from trust to mistrust,
>from generosity to dictatorship!

They take root for life,
become impossible to move,
cement themselves in their positions!
They are surprised
that others also want
their "place in the limelight"
and a chance "to do their own thing"!
In short,
they don't know when to leave!
They have to be uprooted,
their branches cut off...
sometimes very gently,
and then,
they are "put out to grass";
they are by-passed
>(honorary titles,
>jobs without real responsibilities);
sometimes brutally,
and then, it's a regular "unexpected" chopping down
always painful,
>terrifying,
>mortifying.

Warning is given
to all founding fathers and mothers,
to leaders...
who think they are eternal:
"Know when to go.
Don't take root forever.

Leave space for new growth...
The world got along before you arrived.
It will manage to get along after you have gone.
Otherwise,
with the best intentions in the world,
you will become a burden!
You will tyrannize everyone!
You will become a dictator,
whether it be with an iron or velvet glove!
Everyone, except you, will notice it
and suffer from it!
Either openly
or behind your back,
they will let you know
and cut you down!
Know in time
how to become a wise and holy old person
rather than a tyrant and a grouch!''
It is said that a good wine becomes better
as it ages!
There are wines which are almost
a foretaste of heaven.
But, there are some that turn into vinegar:
they give a taste of hell!

It is for your own good that I am going *(Jn 16:7)*.

Unless a wheat grain falls on the ground and dies,
it remains only a single grain *(Jn 12:24)*.

Hoarfrost

I put my face to the window.
Frost had sprinkled it with stars,
thousands of stars,
    long, short,
    small and large,
all fixed on the windowpane.

Sunlight played in each one:
blue stars, yellow, red and green,
shimmered through the white frost.

My window was a garden of stars,
a fairyland of light.
Pure beauty
from the fingers of winter.

God, how beautiful You must be
as You mirror yourself
so beautifully
in Your creation!

Frost and cold, bless the Lord!
give glory and eternal praise to Him.
Ice and snow, bless the Lord!
give glory and eternal praise to Him! *(Dn 3:69-70).*

Failings

The bride was so beautiful
in her lace gown
and bridal veil.
But, at the waist of the dress was a stain,
an ugly stain that nothing could take out;
neither all the mother's skill
nor the strongest detergents,
had been able to remove it.
And it could not be hidden by her wedding bouquet.
Odd — no one saw the beauty of the lacy dress,
nor the glow of the bride.
No one saw further than that wretched stain.
We are made like that, it seems.

He went to the dentist to have a tooth out.
And since then, his tongue keeps going back
to the hole where his tooth had been.
It seems as if his tongue forgets
    the other remaining teeth,
but only remembers the one that is missing.
We are made like that, it seems.

He had every good quality:
polite, pleasant, helpful and more and more.
Only, for some time now, he eats a clove of garlic
every morning ''for his cholesterol''
and everyone avoids him like the plague.
We are made like that, it seems.

* * *

Why do we look at people under a magnifying glass?
Why do we notice the petty side of people
rather than their good qualities?
Why are we so shortsighted
that we see only the failings
rather than their virtues?
Why in our dealing with other people
would we rather do substractions,
whereas in money matters,
we willingly do just the opposite?

O Lord,
teach us to see the good qualities in others
rather than their failings,
to value the positive side of life
rather than let ourselves be overwhelmed
by negative things.
Teach us to see our failings and those of others
as so many shadows
which can make the light seem to shine more brightly.
Help us to see and appreciate that light. *Amen.*

You should carry each other's troubles
and fulfill the law of Christ *(Ga 6:2).*

Treat each other in the same friendly way
as Christ treated you *(Rm 15:7).*

Just a mosquito

Tom was tired.
He worked hard all that day,
so he planned to relax the way he wanted!

It was all worked out.
First thing, he would have a shower,
then read the paper,
smoke a cigar
and watch the news on television.
Then he would go to bed, relax,
and sleep the sleep of the just!

In fact, everything happened according to his plan:
the shower, the news, the cigar.
When Tom went to his bedroom,
he felt just fine,
ready to fall into the arms of Morpheus.
The only problem was that he had not been able
to foresee everything
and it was here
that his plans fell apart.

He was no sooner between the sheets that a mosquito,
just a small mosquito,
began to buzz in his ear.
Tom brushed it off with the back of his hand
and snuggled deeper into the pillow.
He was just on the edge of sleep
when a familiar buzz reached him.
Tom jumped out of bed
as though in the middle of a nightmare,
his hands swinging wildly around his head.

The noise stopped.
Tom, his nerves on edge,
grumbled his way back under the comforter.
But you don't know mosquitoes
if you think they give up so easily.
Tom had just begun to count sheep
when he heard the familiar buzzing.
Tom was suddenly, completely awake.
He decided to finish off this wretched little beast.
He put on the light, found his newspaper
and made a fly swat out of it
and set himself to hunt down this fearsome enemy.
Where the devil could it be?
Tom checked every square inch,
the walls, the ceiling, the floor.
For a whole hour,
rage in his heart,
red hot with fury,
he looked for that wretched mosquito!
But he found nothing, nothing, nothing!
Tired out, irritable, fed up,
Tom stretched out on his bed
and fell asleep.
He woke the next morning
with a beautiful mosquito bite on his left eyelid.

While he had his coffee with bacon and eggs,
Tom thought that perhaps
he should have let himself be bitten
on the first attack
since anyway the result was the same!
At least,
he would have fallen asleep earlier!
Driving to the office,
Tom went on thinking it over.
How many times a day are there "mosquitoes"

which irritate us!
A customer who makes us lose
an hour of our precious time!
A toothache!
Spaghetti which makes your mouth water
and tastes burned!
The person next to you in the theatre
who chews gum
and messes up the whole evening!
The parking ticket stuck on the car
while out to supper!
The flat tire which makes you late!
The gossip who won't stop talking in the phone booth
when you have an urgent call to make!
And so on...!
Tom said to himself:
It's not the big things which hurt us the most.
It's the "mosquitoes" which prick us just enough
to irritate and put us out.
Perhaps we should let ourselves
be "pricked" calmly, patiently,
rather than waste energy
resisting and fighting
and lose the battle anyway.
And Thomas, our steady Thomas, surprised himself
by laughing out loud,
all by himself in his car
and slapped himself on the thigh.

What the Spirit brings is very different:
love, joy, peace, patience, kindness, goodness,
trustfulness, gentleness, and self-control *(Ga 5:22)*.

Be at peace among yourselves *(1 Th 5:14)*.

Kites

When it's the windy season,
it's also the season for kites.

Robert made a kite for himself.
He found thin, light pieces of wood,
a scrap of polythene fabric,
some paper for the tail,
and a long, long string.
And he was ready to challenge the wind.

Robert ran his kite at arms-length
and suddenly his kite began
to climb.
It went up, higher and higher.
Robert fed out more string
and his kite began to dance in the sky.
It pirouetted, it curved,
it turned and circled.
Sometimes, it swooped down.
But always it followed
the whims of the wind.

On the other end of the string,
there was a child,
full of pleasure and delight,
new lord of the sky,
a budding astronaut.

Not far away, adults followed
the tricks of this new bird
and watched

the racing of the child
and found themselves with some surprising thoughts:
''Perhaps we should make kites ourselves,
not make prisons for ourselves everyday!
If we gave free rein to what is best in us,
instead of indulging ourselves in the wrong way!
If we gave ourselves up to the whims of the wind,
the wind of life,
instead of regulating and planning everything!
If we became, a little,
just a little,
like children...''

Let the little children come to me.
Do not stop them!
For it is to such as these
that the kingdom of God belongs *(Mk 10:14).*

For the love of her cats...

She was at the corner of a busy street,
a large empty jar at her side.
She did not ask for money,
but for milk.
Imagine!... Milk!
Passersby looked at her and laughed
and went on their way.
What oddity would have
a pint of milk with him
to give to an old lady on a street corner?

But one morning, a woman felt sorry
for the poor old soul.
— Come, I'll give you some milk.
— Thank you! You are being so good to my cats.
— What? You need milk for your cats?
—Yes, they are thirsty, poor little souls,
   they have had nothing for two days.
— I'm not the Society for the Protection of Animals.
   I'll give for people but not for cats.
   Indignant, she walked quickly round the corner
   leaving the old lady
   more depressed than ever.
   The woman did not understand
   that for the old lady,
   her cats were her only reason for living,
   she had nothing else in her life.

   Maybe it is foolish to give "charity" to animals,
   but, if through them you pick someone up

and bring back some zest for living,
then isn't this real charity, real love?
It should make us think... and act!

Care for the weak and be patient with everyone
(1 Th 5:15).

Oh God...!

I took in my hand
a maple leaf,
just a leaf,
which was on the ground
at the foot of the tree.
Scarlet and purple,
gold and flame coloured,
all the colours of the setting sun.

My eyes saw these colours
and my fingers felt its texture:
     a world of beauty,
     a universe of marvels,
     there in my hands,
     there to my eyes...
Oh God, how beautiful You must be!

I took between my fingers
a rose,
just a small rose,
growing beside a stream,
simply, modestly,
in the wind,
in its dress of beauty.

I turned it around in my fingers.
Every way, it was beautiful.
Chanel and Dior couldn't match its perfume:
     a small wonder,
     between my fingers,
     in my eyes...
Oh God, how glorious You must be!

I took in my arms
a small child,
a very young baby,
who gazed at me,
smiled at me,
weak, fragile,
yet full of life,
rich in promise!
A life just beginning!
The fruit of love!
    there in my arms,
    there in my eyes,
    there in my heart!
Oh God, how You are love and life!

The lonely man

It was in the evening after supper.
The sun was still high
but its rays were less strong.
I was kneeling by my flowerbeds,
working among the flowers.

I did not notice when he came.
He was just standing there beside me,
watching me weed the path.
He must have been about twenty-five.
I had never seen him before...

— Hi! Can I help you?
— No thanks, I just need to be with someone...
— Would you like a cup of coffee? Glass of water?
— No, no, don't talk. Just go on working.
   I just need to be near someone.

I started working again.
He stayed near me.
When I went into the house,
he asked if he could come too.
"Fine", I said.
He sat down in the rocking chair in the kitchen,
and rocked awhile.
I washed my hands and smoked a pipe.
Then suddenly, he stood up, shook my hand
and said: "Thank you very much",
and left.
I don't know where.
Who could know the secret of this young man?

Disappointed in love?
Melancholy? So young!
Unbearably lonely?
Discouraged
or just simple curiosity?
Who knows?
May his time spent with me have helped him
and peace be with him always!

Dinosaurs

Peter is five and a half.
He was watching a television program
on prehistory,
about dinosaurs, brontosaurs, tyrannosaurs
and many other ''saurs''!
There were plenty of them!

Peter has a forty year old uncle
and asked him very seriously:
''Uncle George, did you see those animals
when you were little?''
His uncle laughed loudly and said:
''No, I'm a bit younger than that!''
Then he said to his friend:
''These children don't have any sense of time.
They take us already for tottery old men.
They won't say that when they're as old as we are.''

George has an aunt eighty-nine years old.
Each time he comes back from visiting her,
the same thoughts bounce around his head:
''Aunt Annie is really too old fashioned!
She doesn't fit in with our times,
she's just from another era.
She doesn't understand us.
Really, she's a museum piece!''
The conclusion is easy to see!

The storm

It was unbearably hot.
You could cut the humidity with a knife.
There was no breeze to cool things down.
Dead, heavy weather!
Then clouds piled up in the sky,
hiding the sun.
It was as oppressive as in a funeral parlour.
Dead calm!
The still that comes before the storm.
In the distance, echoed the first rolls of thunder.
Lightning zigzagged across the sky.
The wind rose quickly.
Then the rain began.
Gently at first, then more and more heavily,
the storm fell over us.
A magnificent storm!
For one full hour!

After the storm, the air felt pure and dry:
how good to breathe!
The temperature dropped several degrees:
how well we all felt!
A gentle breeze touched us:
how soft it was!
A rainbow arched over the mountain:
how marvellous!

But after the storm,
we found broken trees, smashed flowers.
Branches bent down to the ground.
A small shed crushed.
Such a pity!

For some days, the atmosphere in the office
had become unbearable.
The boss hid himself behind thick files.
The workers avoided getting in his way.
No jokes, no good stories, no laughter, not a smile!
Just the necessary "work exchanges", formal, cold!
Everyone talked in monosyllables:
Yes, no, thanks, please!
Just as they do on the westerns!

Then, one morning, storm signals showed!
The boss started on his secretary.
She had to retype a letter three times,
because of some "commas".
Then he told off a department head
about a paper
"which should have been on his desk three days ago".
Then, he grumbled that the coffee tasted terrible
and "it doesn't take a college degree
to make decent coffee".
Definitely, it was no time to tread on his toes!
Not only did he look angry!
He was angry!
At lunch, everyone exchanged remarks.
Humorous at first, then angry!
The storm broke during the afternoon coffee break.
It was a magnificent storm.
Anger made the tension rise.
You might think the boss' tie was strangling him.
He was so red faced!
Insults and wisecracks shot around
like thunderbolts,
sarcastic remarks and insults flew
at lightning speed.
They might have come to blows
if the wisest or the more tired

had not quietly slipped out,
leaving the boss fuming by himself.

The next day was spent sorting out the damage
from the storm.
Two employees asked to see the boss,
to hand in their resignations.
His secretary did not come to work.
The boss began to think things over.
He called everyone to a meeting.
He apologized, they apologized;
he said he was wrong,
they said they had made mistakes.
So, in a cooler climate,
they made a list of their complaints
and some possible remedies,
and formed a committee to put forward some solutions.
The secretary came back to work,
there were no resignations,
and life became normal
as on the nicest days of the year.

There are some necessary angers
or at least some useful ones.
Christ himself had a couple
that were pretty good.
There are some which accomplish nothing,
just destroy things and people too.

If you are angry every day
it is as if the weather is always stormy.
That's not normal.
You need to sort yourself out,
my friend.
If, like everyone else, you get upset now and then,
like the weather,

let it be a good anger that clears the loaded air,
but doesn't leave too many broken trees
  on the ground!

If you can negotiate
instead of losing your temper,
settle things peacefully
rather than in an emotional crisis,
be a gentle wind rather than a hurricane,
that's much better!

Happy the gentle,
they shall have the earth for their heritage! *(Mt 5:4).*

Snow

Snow falls,
    white,
    pure,
    spotless.
It comes
    gently,
    slowly,
    silently.
Then suddenly the wind joins the snow.
The weather forecast is zero visibility.
Yet, if you stick your nose to the window pane,
you see such beauty!
Twirls and spirals,
drawn by the wind,
under your fascinated gaze!

And when the wind stops,
you see curves and sculptured shapes,
that the wind has made
    at the corner of the house,
    around a tree,
    in the bed of a stream.

And you say:
the snow is so beautiful!
What artist could make
such delicate shapes out of crystals?
How amazing the wind
which can make such pictures,
draw such lines!

And you go on,
     admiring,
     praising,
     contemplating…

Winds! all bless the Lord,
give glory and eternal praise to Him.
Frost and cold! bless the Lord,
give glory and eternal praise to Him *(Dn 3:65.69).*

A promise

His dad had said to him:
"If you are good,
I will give you a dog."
So David tried to be good:
    he tidied his toys,
    he shut doors quietly,
    he wiped his feet on the doormat,
    he went to bed in time,
and all this for day after day...
but his dad did not give him his dog.

One evening, while his dad was reading his paper,
David said:
— Tell me, dad, haven't you noticed
  how good I have been?
— Yes, my son, you have really improved.
— Don't you remember your promise?
— What promise?
— You said that, if I was good,
  you would give me a dog.
  And you know,
  a promise is a promise;
  it's made to be kept.
— I'll have to think about it.
  Time to go to bed now.

So David went to sleep
with his head full of dreams.
But in his father's head,
that little phrase kept echoing:
"A promise is a promise;

it's made to be kept.''
The next day, he found a pet shop,
a ''shop for dogs'', as David called it.
And since then,
David has had his dog as his friend
and above all, trust in a given word.

Do not let your hearts be troubled.
Trust in God still and trust in Me.
There are many rooms in My Father's house;
if there were not, I should have told you.
I am going now to prepare a place for you,
and after I have gone and prepared you a place,
I shall return to take you with Me;
so that where I am
you may be too *(Jn 14:1-3)*.

So it is with you; you are sad now.
But I shall see you again
and your hearts will be full of joy
and that joy no one shall take from you *(Jn 16:22)*.

Hope

For some time, Francis had been very depressed.
He had the blues, worn out by boredom,
so sad that he felt in the dark.
Despite all he tried,
he could not shake off this depression.

One fall afternoon,
he decided to stroll through the nearby woods
and after a while he stopped near a stream
gurgling gently,
with rustling leaves overhead.

He sat on a rock
and began to beat the ground rhythmically
with the small branch he had been using as a cane.

And, there, in the quiet of the forest,
he marvelled at what he saw...

A squirrel with cheeks full of nuts,
carrying them to his shelter for the winter.
A little black ant pulled pieces of wood
bigger than itself
to his underground house.
He noticed a bee,
splashing about as if drowning in the stream.
''Bit like me'', he said.
But opened his eyes
when he saw a thrush drop a piece of straw
beside the bee!

Francis began to think this over
while some butterflies fluttered lightly around his head.
He leaned back gently against a tree trunk
and slid into a deep sleep.

When he woke up,
the sun had set
and darkness covered the forest with its cloak.
Francis was afraid,
he could see nothing.
What should he do?
He began to shout,
calling for help.
Suddenly he heard a childish voice:
— Sir, have you lost your way?
   Give me your hand,
   I'll guide you out of the forest.
— But you can't see better than I can
   in this dark night.
   How can you help?
— I am blind, Sir.
   The night to me makes no difference.
   I see just as well as in the daytime
   and I know all these paths by heart.
   Don't be afraid.

And that evening,
Francis was saved from the dark night
by a blind youth
who saw much better than he did!

They came to the town
and Francis could see the child's face:
a small urchin with blond hair.
''You see, you don't need to be so sad!
I felt in your hand how hurt you are.

Sadness, you know, is like butterflies.
You must not keep them shut up,
you must let them free."
Joining action to words,
he opened his hands
to let free a blue butterfly.
Then he laughed and ran away.
Francis did not know what to do...
he stood dumbfounded!

II
GOSPEL LIGHTS

I shall walk beside you...

The Lord said to him:
''Don't be afraid.
In all your actions,
in all your roads,
I shall walk by your side.
Trust in me.''

And he undertook all sorts of projects.
He went from success to success.
And, in the evening,
when he thanked God
for the good day he had spent,
he shut his eyes.
Then, as if in a dream,
he saw a path
and, on this path, two sets of footprints.
He said to himself:
''These are the footsteps of the Lord
Who walks with me.''
And he went to sleep, happy,
believing in the promise of his God.

Then, suddenly, things began to go wrong:
failure after failure,
problem after problem.
But what bothered him the most
was that, after his night prayers,
when he shut his eyes,
he still saw the road
but only one set of footprints.

And he said to himself:
"Could it be
that the Lord is no longer at my side?
Could He leave me alone in my anxieties,
that He is not faithful to His promise?"
One night when he prayed,
he dared to ask:
"Where are You, Lord?
I see only one set of footprints.
Have You abandoned me?"
And from the bottom of his heart,
he heard the Lord reply:
"It's true
that there is only one set of footprints.
But they are Mine!
Since you were sick,
since you were sad,
I carried You in My arms!"

Do not be afraid.
I am with you *(Jr 1:8).*

The handwriting of God...

God writes upright,
on the crooked lines of our lives *(Portuguese proverb).*

We read easily the crooked lines,
especially the big happenings
which mark our lives,
make it take new directions.
Sometimes, they come dressed in joy, in happiness:
engagements, weddings, promotions, honours...
But sometimes, they bring sadness, unhappiness:
sickness, grief, separation, unemployment...
They make us or they destroy us.

Looking back over the thread of years,
we can see that each happening has played
a big role in our lives and we also see
that they are linked together,
as if sewn by a master thread.
Looking back, we see
that our lives have been guided,
they have been directed.

Some call it Destiny, Fate,
others say Divine Providence.
It is perhaps the upright writing of God.

Learning to read is an art.
We do not always have prophets at hand
as in former times in Israel.
It is also a grace
which must be asked of God.

To read the upright lines in our lives
through the curved ones,
is to discover the will of God
which is unwearying love
for each one of us.

I love you with an everlasting love *(Jr 31:3).*

It is Christmas

Is it Christmas in everyone's heart?
Is it Christmas in the heart of
        the sick,
        the elderly,
        the orphan,
        the widow?
Is it Christmas in the heart of
        the unemployed,
        the outcast,
        the abandoned,
        the prisoners?
Is it Christmas in the heart of
        the tortured
        the exiled,
        the refugees,
        the handicapped,
        the unloved?

Christmas is
        a smile to someone in pain,
        a hand held out to pick someone up,
        an open wallet for someone starving...
Christmas is
        when you share your shelter
                with someone homeless,
        when you give your food to the hungry,
        when you give your coat to the poor...
Christmas is
        drying the tears of a child,
        your hand in the hand
        of a bewildered blind person,
        your kiss to the old man in a home...

It is Christmas in people's hearts,
each time
     coercion is changed into freedom,
     power becomes service,
     authority becomes humility...
each time
     tenderness goes with love,
     gentleness is added to devotion,
     kindness holds the hand that serves...
each time
     peace replaces war,
     giving replaces profits,
     joy wins over sadness...

You make Christmas,
if you open
     your eyes to contemplate,
     your hands to give,
     your heart to love...
if you share
     your bread with those poorer than yourself,
     your time with those who are busy,
     your smile with those who are sad...
if you can
     forgive,
     sow joy,
     help lighten a grief...

I dream
     of a white Christmas,
     of a joyful Christmas,
     of a shared Christmas!

Come...

Would you taste spring water
that will always refresh you?
Would you walk without being tired?
Would you have nights full of light?
Would you taste love which is unchangeable?
Would you always desire and yet be satisfied?
Would you possess everything and lose nothing?
Would you love and be loved without misgiving?
Is this what you want?

Then, come with Me.
Take My hand.
Be not afraid.
Lean on Me.
Do not look behind you.
Leave behind the things that hold you.
Come, follow Me.
You find the road hard?
Believe Me!
He who walks with Me does not stumble.
I am with you...
I will never abandon you.
Believe Me!
I love you!

At the end of the road
and even on the way,
if you hold My hand always,
you shall see the never failing light,
you shall have endless knowledge,
you shall love without limit
and you shall live, live... always, always!

Do not be afraid of them,
for I am with you
to protect you *(Jr 1:8)*.

Go and sell everything you own
and give the money to the poor
and you will have treasure in heaven!
Then come, follow me! *(Mk 10:21)*.

The splinter and the plank

Joan laughed inwardly at Sue
because Sue's false eyelashes had come off
    her eyelids,
and her mascara was running down her cheeks.
Yet Joan hadn't noticed
that her own slip was longer than her skirt,
and one of her stockings was inside out!

Tom thought that Joe was to be pitied.
Sometimes Joe had to ask for credit
at the grocery store.
Yet Tom did not realize what a huge amount
he paid on his car every month!

Charlie was fed up:
he had found a teenager stealing nails
from his hardware store
and had practically chased him out of the place:
"Don't let me ever see you here again!"
But, that very day, he increased
the price of his patio paving stones
by fifty per cent!
He said to the cashier who pointed out
that he had put up the price the week before:
"It's the time of year to sell paving stones
and I just have to look after myself.
People will buy just the same, you'll see!"

Why do you observe the splinter
in your brother's eye
and never notice the plank in your own?

63

How can you say to your brother:

Brother, let me take out the splinter
that is in your eye
when you cannot see the plank in your own?
Hypocrite! Take the plank out of your own eye
and then you will see clearly enough
to take out the splinter
that is in your brother's eye *(Lk 6:41-42).*

To forgive...

You know, as I do,
people who give
    their money
    their belongings,
    their time.
They have a way of making us
    admire them,
    envy them.
They attract us.
Someone who gives,
that's just great!

You know, as I do,
some people who GIVE OF THEMSELVES:
    affection,
    gentleness,
    kindness,
    goodness,
    health.
They don't hesitate
to forget themselves,
sacrifice their interest,
for something they're interested in,
for people whom they love.
To give... that's great!
To give oneself... that's even
    better,
    but harder,
    more difficult.
People who give themselves,
    challenge us,

      disturb us,
      call us.
I love, I respect the people who give,
but I love and respect even more the people
who give themselves.

There is much more...
      is it possible?
But even then there are people who PARDON,
who shut
      their eyes,
      their ears,
      their mouths,
on any harm done to them,
but who never close
      their hands
      nor their hearts!
These people are not just great or good,
they have something of God about them.
And that is what is good above all!
Love has no boundaries!
      it gives,
      it gives of itself
      it forgives,
      it draws us to it...

God is Love *(1 Jn 4:8).*

You must therefore be perfect
just as your Heavenly Father is perfect *(Mt 5:48).*

The cross...

We have to take up our cross,
or it will take us!
It is no good trying to get away,
it will find us sooner or later.
If we do not accept it,
it will crush us.
If we lie on it,
it will redeem us.

A certain Jesus,
the evening of a certain Friday,
had to choose:
Himself or the cross.
Leaning on it and on his Father,
He was saved the morning
of a certain Sunday.

For God's foolishness is wiser
than human wisdom,
and God's weakness is stronger than
human strength *(1 Cor 1:25).*

But, for him who believes in Him
Who can do all things,
Who can even snatch one from the dead,
that is wisdom!
If we lean on the cross
and on Jesus,
we too, shall be saved!

If anyone wants
to be My follower
let him renounce himself
and take up his cross every day
and follow Me *(Lk 9:23)*.

Was it not ordained
that the Christ should suffer
and so enter into His glory? *(Lk 24:26)*.

He was crucified through weakness
and still He lives now
through the power of God.
So then, we are weak
as He was,
but we shall live with Him
through the power of God *(2 Cor 13:4)*.

I want to be a saint

Lord,
despite
    my heedlesness,
    my wild oats,
    my sins,
You know that,
with all my being,
I want to be a saint.

But!
On one hand,
I try
    to do good,
    to pray well,
    to be useful to others,
    in short, to be a good Christian,
and on the other hand,
I find I am stuck with
    my bad temper,
    my selfishness,
    my pride,
    and my cowardice.
I try to correct myself,
to improve,
yet it really seems to me that I get worse!

Lord, how hard it is to be a saint!

''My son, you want to be a saint, bravo!
But you're not going about it in the right way.

You want to be a saint
in your way
according to your ideas.
You have put yourself to the job,
and that's good.
But, up to now,
you have been steering the boat to holiness
and it's not surprising
that you're not going very fast!

Let Me do it.
Trust Me.
Do not hold against the people and events
that I put on your way.
Don't you see that it is I
Who am weaving the web of your life?
Why do you spend time undoing the thread
that I patiently spin
in the fabric of your days?
Let Me direct things.
You will not fall,
if you put your hand in Mine
and step in My path.
Love
    gently,
    blindly,
    passionately.
It is clear that sometimes
    you will go where you don't want to go,
    you will love in a way you hadn't thought of,
    you will do things that will surprise you.
But you will see how My peace will fill you,
    through success or defeats,
    health or sickness,
    recognition or disaster,
    good or bad times.

Then,
    without your realizing,
    without your being aware of it,
you will become a saint.
You know, holiness is My business,
it's My concern!
All you have to do
is to abandon yourself to Me,
all the days of your life.

Come to Him...

Oh you,
who are oppressed by work,
come!
Come to Him!
for He is all rest!

Oh you,
who suffer from despair,
come!
Come to Him,
for He is all hope!

Oh you,
who weep from grief,
come!
Come to Him,
for He is all comfort!

Oh you,
who are twisted by sorrow,
come!
Come to Him,
for He can soothe you!

Oh you,
who are worn out by loneliness,
come!
Come to Him,
for He is all friendship!

Oh you,
who suffer from worry,
come!
Come to Him,
for He is all peace!

Oh you,
who are hungry, thirsty,
hurt, bruised,
worn out
bewildered,
come!
Come to Him,
    come without fear,
    without hesitation,
    without regret!
Come!

For He is
    the spring that quenches thirst,
    the fire that purifies
    the oasis that refreshes,
    the light that shines out.

We are in His hand.
Our names are written on His palm.
He has looked at us.
He will never abandon us!

Come to Me,
all you who labour
and are overburdened
and I will give you rest...
You will find rest for your souls *(Mt 11:28-29).*

It is enough to love...

His work was never-ending!
He was at every congress,
at every meeting!
He took part on open line radio shows,
and on television interviews!
He had something to say
on nearly everything!
He always had ten irons in the fire.
    A real live wire!

Everyone wanted him,
for this or for that.
He took on everything,
to serve,
but also to be known,
to be recognized.
He never stopped,
always very busy,
too busy.
He runs here, he runs there!
To the right, the left!
In front, behind!
    a real weathercock!

He wanted
    to see all,
    have all,
    know all,
    possess all!
He wanted to be everywhere.
He wanted to have

everything in his hands!
    a real little monster!

What good did he achieve
in this mad running about?
It is not those who rush about
who automatically do any good.
Oh! No!
It is those who love
whether they are active or not.
That was how the Lord wanted it!
So, why are we waiting to love?

Brethren, in your life, put on love above all things
(Col 3:14).

Even though
    I talk in tongues…
    I have the gift of prophecy…
    I have faith in all its fullness…
    I give away all my possessions…
        to the poor…
But am without love,
    I am simply a gong booming…
    I am nothing…
    I gain nothing! *(1 Cor 13:1-2).*

In vain, you get up earlier,
and put off going to bed,
sweating to make a living,
since He provides for His beloved
as they sleep *(Ps 127:2).*

III
PRAYERS

Morning prayer

Lord, a new day is beginning
with its joys and difficulties,
with its successes and defeats.

My mind is filled with projects
and my heart is filled with love.
I know, having had it happen so many times,
that I will not realize half my plans
nor will I love half as much as I would like…

Bless all that I might do
and forgive my indolence
or my too great ambition.
May the love that I'll give today
be unselfish
and forgive me, in advance,
the weakness of my feelings.

Give me enough faith to see You
in my brothers and sisters
and give them enough hope
to seek You in me.

Let me be, today,
an instrument of Your peace,
that I may work for You
in all I do and say.
Lord, bless my day.

Amen.

You...

Let me meet You,
Lord,
as You already reach Your hand to me!

Let me see You face to face
in all Your beauty and splendour,
You, Who already give me hints of Yourself!

Draw me to You,
as the magnet draws the iron,
as the lover draws the loved one!

You intoxicate and bewitch me!
You tempt me, and invite me!
You want me and call me!

May my path be Yours!
May Your will be mine!
May my road be Yours!

Yes,
You Who love me beyond what I can imagine,
You Who know me better than I know myself,
You Who know my needs better than I do,
keep me in Your love!

Amen.

A simple prayer

Lord,
You know me
better than I know myself!
You know what there is in me,
     that is good,
     less good,
     no good.
Only You can sort it out.

Draw me into Your love!
Purify me in Your goodness!
Come close to me,
so that I may be close to You
and close to others!
And may Your peace and joy be always with me!

Prayer before work

God our Father,
to us who are Your children,
You granted enough trust
to make us responsible
for the world that You have made
and our earthly brothers.

In the beginning of this day,
may only concern for Your love
guide us,
may only interest for Your kingdom
enlighten us,
may only action for the good
of our brothers and sisters,
be our aim.

May your Son, Jesus, be with us
each moment, on the paths of this day.
May Your Holy Spirit
give us His light
and His strength.
May He pacify us and let us bring peace.
May He give us His joy.

Through our smile and our greeting,
may the people, who meet us today,
see Your goodness, Your tenderness, Your love.
And, in turn, may we see You
in their looks and hopes.

Amen.

Prayer

Lord,
> I wish I were as patient as George
> but so many times I am angry,
> sometimes even violent.

Lord,
> I wish I were as straightforward as Suzie,
> but sometimes I get these phony ideas
> and You'd think I was someone else!

Lord,
> I wish I were as handy as Al,
> but I have trouble sawing straight
> and can hardly hammer in a nail
> > without bending it.

Lord,
> I wish I were as cheerful as Ann,
> but I seem to be uptight so often
> and sometimes I'm downright mean!

Lord,
> I wish I could work like Peter,
> but I like doing nothing much,
> and I fritter time away...

Lord,
> I wish, I wish, there is no end
> of telling you that I would like...

Lord,
 Let me praise the good I see in others,
 change what can be changed in me,
 let me accept and love myself as I am,
 because You, You love me as I am!

Amen.

I saw You...

Lord, what shall I tell You?
I saw You
    in that patient in the hospital
    who needed some attention from me...
And it was You Who questioned me!

I saw You
    in that lonely person,
    who knocked at my door,
    looking for company...
And it was You Who called upon me!

I saw You
    in that worker for the Third World,
    who gives his life
    to look after those who suffer...
And it was You Who disturbed me!

I saw You
    in that contemplative nun
    who gives her whole life
    to pray to You...
And it was You Who fascinated me!

I saw You
    in that mother of a family
    who lost her health caring for her children...
And it was You Who entranced me!

I saw You
    in that poor man who asked for no money

but gave me the riches of his heart
in his smile...
And it was You Who delighted me!

Lord, I was used to seeing You
in the consecrated bread
and to adore You,
to pray to You
now and again.
But, it didn't reach through my comfortable,
feather-soft life.
I could serve You
while still looking after myself
and manage to harmonize both.

But, since I saw You
in the faces
of the poor,
of the weak,
of the destitute,
in the lives of those given to You
completely,
directly,
or to the poor,
which is about the same,
I do not sleep so peacefully.

It is not self-reproach but a call
which I feel rise within me,
a call which becomes ever louder.
Sometimes, I wish I could stop my ears,
but deep inside me, in the depths,
I know You.
I know that from now on
I could never evade
Your glance.
I could not wish not to see You again.

You have called me
    bewitched me,
    shaken me.
You have held me...
    seduced me...
I shall not resist
    your pressing invitation
    your love,
    your look.
I saw You,
You conquered me!
I saw You,
I will not leave You!
I saw You,
I shall never grow tired of You!
Let me only
    feel Your hand hold mine,
    Your footsteps go before me,
    and Your heart warm mine.

Amen.

''Lord, when did we see You hungry and feed You?
Or thirsty and give You drink?
When did we see You a stranger
    and make You welcome,
naked and clothe You,
sick or in prison and go to see You?''
And the King will answer:
''I tell you solemnly,
in so far you did this
to one of the least of these brothers of mine,
you did it to me'' (Mt 25:40).

Prayer of a dissatisfied man

Lord, I am never satisfied,
not even able to be satisfied.
I find fault with everything, everyone.
I grumble all the time.
I complain too easily.

I am given flowers...
they're not the colour I wanted!
Someone phones to know how I am...
it's not convenient to talk to them!
Someone visits me...
they put me out!
No one visits me...
everyone has forgotten me!

Lord, why do I act this way?
    why has life made me like this?
    why is my love inside out?
    why can't I be tender?
    why do I always have to look
    on the worse side?
I am unable to give a hand,
    a smile,
    a hug.
I seem as surly as a bear.
I'm as prickly as a porcupine.
I'm as wild as a wolf.

Lord, no one loves me
since I am unable to love them.
You know that, somewhere behind my crabby exterior,

I have a good heart.
If my bark is tough,
my heart is tender.
But I can't show it,
no one knows…
It hurts so much.

I beg You
for those I treat so roughly,
for those who go on loving me,
despite everything.
I don't ask You to make me pleasant down here,
You can't straighten out an old tree
without breaking it.
But when I am with You in Paradise,
then You will show openly what today I cannot show,
     my generosity,
     my tenderness,
     my kindness,
     my love.

Amen.

Prayer of the abandoned

Lord,
You Who had pity
in your tenderness
for that widow who had just lost
her only son!

You, Who helped, as a friend,
Martha and Mary who had lost
their brother, Lazarus!

You, Who gave back courage to Jairus
who had lost his little daughter!

You, Who brought back hope to the centurion
who had lost his servant!

You, Who made your mother live again
who was going to lose you...!

We beg You,
do not leave us.
Give us fresh courage, strength, hope.
Keep us in your kindness, tenderness and love.
Lead us on the paths
of sharing, brotherhood, friendship.
May we never be alone, again!

Amen.

Weariness

Lord,
I do not know where I am going...
I go round in circles,
I just mark time.
Everything was going well,
I enjoyed working,
plenty of plans.
I was full
of enthusiasm for living, creating...
And then, it was just
as if something had hit me on the head...
My health broke down!
How true it is
that troubles never come singly!

Here I am before You,
    empty,
    reduced to nothingness,
    no enthusiasm,
    no taste for work.
I am looking for myself!
I Look for You.
Where are You taking me?
What is in Your heart for me?
Let me recognize You in the ways of my life,
let me carry my cross with Yours,
let me find out what You expect of me in this tunnel.
And may Your will be done!

Amen.

Evening family prayer

Lord,
the day is coming to its close,
it is already late,
and night is spreading over the earth.

Having gone through the day doing our best,
we are once again gathered 'neath the same roof,
in the midst of our family.

Before retiring for the night,
we want to say "Thank You" for this day.
Surely, nothing was perfect.
    For our failings,
    for our selfishness,
    for our cowardice,
we ask Your forgiveness,
because we are sure of Your love,
and strong in Your goodness!

For our acts of tenderness,
    our attentiveness
    and our tactfulness,
we praise You
and give You thanks.

Fill us with Your love,
keep us in Your peace,
protect us from sadness
and be our rest both day and night!

Amen.

Evening prayer

Lord,
> here I am before You this evening
> at the end of another working day.

Take any good I have done,
> and give it life,
as for the evil I have done,
let Your unwearying mercy flow over it.

On those of my brothers whom I have hurt today
> place the warmth of Your tenderness,
> over those I have misjudged
> stretch the shadow of Your peace.

To those who helped me spend this day
> give them joy,
to those who have smiled at me,
> lavish the gentleness of Your spirit.

May Your love be with us all,
> in this night that You give us,
and may that, in the depths of our sleep,
> Your light shine on us.

Amen.

A prayer before sleeping

Lord,
it is late.
Already,
darkness spreads over the earth.
Another day has ended,
      with its joys and troubles,
      with its success and failures,
      with its hopes and despairs.
We place all these in Your heart.
Lord,
it's big enough to welcome everything!

We offer You
      what we did that was good,
      what we succeeded in,
      what we have loved.
We beg You to forgive
      our weakness,
      our lack of love,
      our selfishness.

Bless our sleep
that it may be calm and untroubled,
so that tomorrow we may be ready again
to love You
in our brothers and sisters in this world.

Amen.

IV
REFLECTIONS

If...

If it has always been easy for you,
     you will never understand those
     who find it hard to live...
You have to find what is difficult...
     That's important.

If you have never risked anything,
     refusing to take chances,
     hanging on to what is certain,
you will never understand those who gamble
     with their lives...
You have to practice taking risks...
     That's important.

If you have never known suffering
     except in books, or in other people,
you will never understand what it is
     to groan with pain...
You have to welcome suffering when it comes...
     That's important.

If you have never known defeat,
     if you are perfect,
you will never understand those
     who have been defeated by life...
You have to be in the same boat as the weak...
     That's important.

If you have never been lacking
        in the necessities of life,
        but filled up with bonds and shares and
            a well paid job,
you will never understand what it is
        to live from day to day...
You must become poor in something or in someone...
        That's important.

It's too easy to understand with the head!
        Then you don't really understand.
We really understand only with our hearts
        and our hands.
The rest is vanity and illusion.

His state was divine,
yet He did not cling
to His equality with God,
but emptied Himself
to assume the condition of a slave
and became as men are;
and being as all men are,
He was humbler yet even to accepting death,
death on a cross.
But God raised Him on high... *(Ph 2:6-9).*

A full life...

To have a full life!
Everyone wants that.
What does it mean?

A well filled wallet?
International fame?
Real power?
To be healthy all one's life?

Did you ever think that a full life is
above all
a matter of the heart?

If your heart is full
    of help given,
    of sharing done,
    of forgiveness,
    of constant availability...
If your heart is
    in your hands,
    in your head,
    in your feet...
If your heart knows how
    to give its time,
    spend its energy...
If your heart becomes
    the tender look,
    the attentive listener,
    the life giving word...
If your heart can
    encourage, stimulate,

give energy,
suffer, console...

If your heart can
    laugh and cry,
    sing and shout,
    talk or be silent...
Then your life is full,
    whether your wallet is flat or not,
    whether your name is in the paper or not,
    whether you are powerful or weak,
    whether you are sick or healthy!

We only see clearly with the eyes of the heart;
the essential things are invisible! *(Saint-Exupéry).*

May God enlighten the eyes of our mind... *(Ep 1:18)*

Look... listen...

Have you ever taken time
to look at a flower,
an ordinary flower...?
  Its amazing colour,
  its individual shape,
  its subtle perfume,
  its simple beauty,
  its unspoken language,
  its hidden message...
Really, have you ever ''wasted'' time on a flower?

Think of the flowers
growing in the fields:
I assure you that not even Solomon in all his regalia
was robed like one of these *(Mt 6:28-29).*

Have you ever stopped to listen
and to look at the laugh of a child?
  Its incomparable melody,
  its matchless colour,
  its clear purity,
  its transparency...
Did you ever really have your heart
won by the laugh of a child?

Let the little children come to me
and do not stop them
for it is to such as these
that the kingdom of Heaven belongs *(Lk 18:16).*

Have you ever watched the look
on an old man's face?

His watchful tenderness,
his unchangeable serenity,
his extraordinary humility,
his silent wisdom...
Really, have you ever watched the look
on the face of an old man?

You are to rise up before gray hairs,
you are to honor old age and fear your God.
I am Yahweh *(Lv 19:32)*.

Yes, it isn't lost time
to look at
a flower,
a sunset,
the grace of young girls,
the strength of young men,
the devotion of a mother,
the work of a mature man,
the wrinkled face of the old.
Look and look again,
look, admire!
Look and wonder,
look and contemplate!
Yes, take time to hear
the laugh of a child,
the song of birds,
the rush of the wind,
the fall of rain,
the sound of a lullaby,
the pattern of a symphony.

Listen and listen again.
Listen and be amazed.
Listen and be glad.
Listen and you will be exalted...

Your wonder and your joy
will fill you with hope
and take away all hint of suffering.
And, who knows,
but at the end of your contemplation
and ecstasy,
that you will not be favoured by Life,
overwhelmed by Love,
that you will not meet Him?

Balance...

You're balanced,
if you don't fall!
You sit comfortably in your armchair:
you're balanced.
You walk or climb a stair:
you're balanced.
And yet the difference is enormous.
In your chair, you're not going forward.
On the stair, you're climbing.
Scientists say that balance is either
        static (the chair)
        or dynamic (the staircase).

Life is always a matter of dynamic balance,
since it always moves forward.
When you walk or climb a stair,
have you noticed that you are always
on one foot?
If you don't lift one foot,
if you don't take the risk of being off-balance,
if you're not brave enough to try,
if you have no confidence in your ability
to find a new balance,
to go forward,
you will stay rooted in one spot!
Life is full of risks, of daring, of trust!
It is the price of growth!

If it were not true...

Lord, I have spent my life,
my long life,
believing in You
and in the teaching of Your Church.
I have tried to love You
the best I could.
I didn't always do so well
but I know that You understand.
But now, at the end of my life,
I feel full of doubts.
I don't see things so clearly:
if it were not true...
Suppose I have done all these things
for nothing:
     Lenten fasts,
     Friday without meats,
     rosaries,
     Sunday mass,
     regular confession...
Religion has changed so much:
     fasting is forgotten,
     we eat meat on Fridays,
     people don't go to Mass,
     there seem to be no more sins!
I don't seem to know what is true, what is good.
I am so mixed up
and then I get worried,
You know!

* * *

"My child,
it's true.
Things have changed a lot
since you were young;
and I do understand
that you don't always know
just where you stand.
But let Me say:
you didn't do everything for nothing.
Across the practices of your time,
you wanted
    to love Me,
    to reach out to Me,
and that is what matters.
Don't worry.
There are many ways of loving
and each time has its own.
You don't have to compare,
even judge
and condemn.
The most important thing is to love.
You have loved
and you continue loving.
Be at peace!
You have put your hand
in the hand I offered you
and I keep it tight against My heart."

What is it good for...?

What is the good of being powerful
    if you crush the weak?
What is the good of knowledge
    if you use it to deceive the ignorant?
What is the good of being rich
    if you make the poor more wretched?

Power is given,
not to enslave others
    but to serve!
Knowledge is given,
not for oneself
    but for others!
Riches are given,
not to heap up money
    but to share!

He has pulled down princes from their thrones
and exalted the lowly! *(Lk 1:52).*

He has filled the hungry with good things,
the rich sent empty away *(Lk 1:53).*

Light...

Light...!
We are so used to seeing it...
That we are hardly aware of it.
We don't appreciate
     its wonders,
     its blessings.
We seem blind in full daylight.

Yet, how can we become used
to the dawn
     that comes back each morning?
To the glancing sunshine
     that breaks through the high cloud or the forest?
To brightness through the shadows?

Surely we value
     the light which
     brightens the nights,
     the lamp which helps us find our way,
     the lighthouse which guides shipping.

I have a blind friend
who never stops telling me:
"You don't know how lucky you are!"
Discover light again!
Be seekers for the light,
to radiate light!

And Jesus said to the people:
     "I am the light of the world!

Anyone who follows Me
will not be walking
in the dark.
He will have the light of life'' *(Jn 8:12)*.

God said:
    ''Let there be light'',
    and there was light.
    God saw that light was good *(Gn 1:3)*.

Your light must shine in the sight of men *(Mt 5:16)*.

A child

When you consider...

What's the strength of a child?
    It is his weakness!
What is the charm of a child?
    It is his openness!
We love a child
because he is without calculation.
We want the best for a child
since he is all promise.

Yes,
    when we think of it...
    We are God's children! *(1 Jn 3:1).*

Look ahead...

He was getting
    old,
    bitter,
    disappointed,
    disillusioned.

He spoke only
    of regrets,
    of complaints,
    of angry remarks.

To listen to him,
his life had been full
    of things he had been forced to do,
    of situations he had not chosen,
    of decisions other people had made for him.

Apparently,
he had only unhappy memories,
he had never done
what he himself wanted to do,
he had always acted against his wishes.

He blamed it on
    his parents,
    his wife,
    his children,
    the neighbours,
    everybody.

He had always been
    manipulated,
    exploited,
    made fun of.

Often he said:
    "I wish I could die...
    I've had enough of this life...
    If I had to live my life over,
    I'd do things differently...
    I've never been happy...
    If I had known...
    I should have..."

Yet he was in good health,
    he walked each day,
    he read the paper,
    he smoked his pipe
    while watching his program.
His children, his grandchildren
and his great grandchildren
visited him regularly,
brought him presents,
remembered his special days...

But he had always been the sort
that says:
"My bottle is half empty",
and everyone wished
he were the sort to say:
"My bottle is half full!"

Lord,
help us
to accept and love people
as they are.

112

Help us to understand them.
You, You love them as they are,
and You know them better than we do.
Yet, help us
to find the positive side
of life and people
that may add light
rather than put it out.

Amen.

Truly it is right and just
to give you thanks
always and everywhere,
O God, almighty Father *(Preface of the Mass).*

113

Struggles

The worst enemies
we meet in life
are not those from outside;
those we call
        competitors,
        jealous people,
        hypocrites,
        liars,
or angry,
        spiteful people,
        flatterers,
        scoffers...

No, the worst enemies
are those within.
They are called
        pride,
        stubborness,
        blindness,
        selfishness,
        conceit,
or despair,
        despondency,
        lack of restraint,
        cowardice,
        laziness...
Against all these,
only God can help us!

Blessed be Yahweh, my rock,
who retains my hands for war
and my fingers for battle.
He is my love, my bastion,
my citadel, my savior *(Ps 144:1-2)*.

Time

Now,
in this day just ended,
have you taken time
    to look closely at a flower,
    to listen joyfully to a child,
    to look lovingly at an old person?

Have you found time
    to take care of yourself,
    to do something for others,
    to pray to your Lord?

Have you lost time
    in working for nothing,
    in serving others,
    in taking some moments of leisure?

No?
You did not have time
    to take time,
    to find time,
    to lose time?

You are busy?
Too many things to do?
You are always in a rush?
You run after time?
You have so much work and so little time?
There isn't time to lose time!
You must rather make time.

Well, my friend,
   it's time more than ever
   that you find time in your life
   for impractical things,
   for things that are free,
   even inefficient, at first sight.
And you will find you still have time
for everything else.

Time is so precious,
we must not waste it.
Time is given to us,
to use well
not to burn and burn us with it.
Time passes.
It never comes back.
Take it.
Grasp it then!

There is a season for everything,
a time for every occupation under heaven *(Ec 3:1).*

Patience...

Are you going to mess up your day
and those working with you,
just because coming to the office
a truck cut you off,
and a woman driving in front of you,
didn't drive the same way you do?

A little patience and calm!
Your nerves and your blood pressure
will do better!
Your co-workers too!

Bear with one another charitably,
in complete selflessness,
gentleness and patience *(Ep 4:2).*

To change one's mind...

Susan is like a sledgehammer,
she is as stubborn as a mule.
My mind's made up about that:
I have known her too long
to change my opinion about her!

Mark is selfish and ambitious.
I have known him a long time:
he'll never change.
With me, he doesn't have any chance.
He is filed and catalogued for life!

The Browns were always liars.
It's well known.
And Harry is a Brown.
So he is a liar naturally,
like all the Browns.
In my eyes, he could hardly be otherwise!

However, and this is what is bothering me,
Susan keeps telling me
how hard she is trying to improve.
I see Mark helping others
and Harry never stops swearing
that he is telling the truth.
I don't understand a thing.

Could it be that these people
whom I have
        judged,
        catalogued,

        condemned,
could they really change?
Must I change my mind about them?

Lord, give me the strength
to change my mind about people.
Let me be able,
not to judge them once for all
but to give them a chance.
Let me find out
that they too can change
and that I must readjust my ideas
from time to time.
Let me be understanding and tolerant,
remembering that I will be judged
in the same measure
that I have judged others.

Amen.

Greatness

To be great,
you don't need
    to own castles,
    to rule over people,
    to possess all knowledge,
    to sail every sea
    or to go to the moon.

The paths to greatness
are open to all,
especially to ordinary people.

You are great
    each time you forget your own advantage
        and help someone else;
    each time you close your eyes
        but not your heart
        to someone who has hurt you;
    each time your tenderness
        brightens someone's morning;
    each time you go to the limit
        of your devotion;
    each time you pursue an ideal
        without flagging;
    each time you courageously pick yourself up
        from a fall;
    each time the warmth in your eyes
        warms up another's life;
    each time you welcome those
        who need you.

Indeed, you are great
     when you are good to others,
     when you are tolerant,
     when you give,
     when you love.
I can tell you
that I know
mothers who are greater than any Head of State,
because they count neither their time
nor their self sacrifice.
There are girls and young men greater than princes,
because their generosity
and gift of themselves
are so admirable;
constant sinners greater than pious people,
because of their trust
in the mercy of God
and their efforts to pick themselves up
go on endlessly.
These and many like them
are great people.
God is seen as wonderful
through them
and their names are written in the Book of Life.

Anyone who wants to become great among you
must be your servant,
and anyone who wants to be first among you
must be slave to all *(Mk 10:43-44)*.

Blindness

Have you noticed that there are two occasions
when you can see nothing?
The first one is
when you are in complete darkness,
that's well known.
But the other happens
when you are in too bright a light!
When you look directly at the sun,
you see nothing:
you are blinded!

So, we are blind either
     in total darkness
     or in absolute light.
Seeing is not found in the extremes.
It exists in the in-between.
Neither too much, nor too little
of light or of darkness.

No one has the whole truth, complete knowledge!
No one is completely ignorant either!
And if you find on your way
someone who believes himself to be
all light or all darkness,
he will see nothing.

Lord, enlighten our dark nights
and put shadow with our sunshine!
Lord, let us see the light
which is in each man
whether it be a lantern
or a searchlight!

Lord, let it be that we are never dazzled,
    that we always have light,
    that we may never blind others,
    that we always give light.
You Who are calm light and gentle shade!

Amen.

A giant elm

Near my home
a giant elm lords it
over the flat countryside.
It is like an immense flower,
a giant bouquet,
at the end of a powerful but peaceful trunk!
It is a wonder
    of harmony,
    of beauty,
    of pride!

And such balance!
It stands on one foot!
But it also possesses what we do not see:
roots!
When your head is sixty feet high,
you need solid footing
and staunch roots.
Botanists say that the roots reach out
as widely as the branches,
and pioneers who had to clear and burn trees
knew what it was to grub up an elm!
The trunk is the balance and the bridge
between the two clusters,
one in the air,
the other, underground.
And with these two extremities,
this giant feeds itself.
The leaves make a synthesis of the light:
''Chlorophyl'', say the scientists,
and the roots draw organic matter
from the soil.

Life unfolds
in every way
in this beauty.
The tree grows
from the outside
as well as from the inside.
It flourishes
from the invisible
and the visible.
Without leaves, no tree!
Without roots, no tree!
Without a trunk to join them, no tree!
It's a magnificent work of art
that generous nature gives us.

The life of men
would gain
from being like my great elm.
The greater the leaf development,
the greater need for deep roots.
The more active the man,
the greater need for contemplation.
It's great to shine before everyone
in the dazzle of action.
But, at the same time, in the organic darkness
of his room or church,
he must go back
to the juice of study and prayer.
And always in balance!

If we concentrate on doing things,
we shall produce beautiful leaves
for a while but we shall end
by fading,
drying up,
and our leaves will fall
for we shall come up as if from concrete!

126

In the same way, unless we are seekers,
contemplatives
or invalids,
we are not made to study and meditate
the whole day long:
we are not only roots.
We have to show what we are
in the world
in the service of our brothers.

It's all a matter of balance!
    Work and study...
    Action and contemplation...
    Work and rest...
    Solitude and social life...
Balance is life.
We have to look for it,
remake it!
It's the price we pay
to make our lives
into something beautiful!

Intolerance!

And Christ said:
    "Happy are the pure of heart!"
And then He talked to Mary Magdalene, the prostitute,
and to the woman taken in adultery.
And the pure were shocked!

And Christ said:
    "You cannot serve God and money!"
And then He dined with Zacchaeus, the tax collector,
and with Simon, the publican,
and with Levi in the custom house.
And people didn't understand anything!

And Christ said:
    "The Son of Man has come to save
    that which is lost...
    I came not for the healthy
    but for the sick and the sinners!"
And He condemned the bigotry of the proud Pharisee
and pitied the weakness of the sincere publican.

And the "pious" people, shocked, said to others:
"You're not ashamed
to meet those who are divorced,
talk to drug addicts,
wave to those homosexuals,
spend an evening with the blacks,
visit those radicals...
I do not understand...
I thought better of you than that."

Lord,
deliver us from intolerance,
heal us from misunderstanding,
keep us from judging,
preserve us from condemning...

Amen.

Details

If you throw a stone in a well,
you set off a real little storm.
Look at the eddies you make;
the ripples come and go,
rebound,
interact,
gradually weaken.

If you threw the same stone in the river,
it wouldn't raise much disturbance,
the river would just go flowing on
calmly.

If you shout at the top of your voice
in your house,
everyone is bothered,
asks about it,
asks you about it.
You put people out.
You shout in the stadium and no one notices:
it's just normal!

Like most of us
you must live in a small community,
one of family, school,
religious group or other;
so, pay attention to details:
those are the things
which make life
bearable or unbearable.

You don't smile at someone…
and life is miserable for him.
You bang the door regularly
and your neighbour gets red in the face about it.
You blow your nose as if it were a trombone
and everyone is mad.
You drink your soup noisily
and everyone rushes to finish their meal.
You must be first to snatch the newspaper,
everyone thinks you're a grabber.
You always take the best chair for the TV,
all say you think only of yourself.
You can finish with your own little list…
whether they are pinpricks or sabrecuts!

But…
You smile at breakfast,
and the day has a good start.
You give a hand with the chores,
and everyone thinks you are helpful.
You light the fire after supper,
and everyone enjoys it.
Sometimes, you play cards with a poor player,
and you make a friend.
You kiss your wife coming back from work,
and your home feels warmer.
You can go on with the list
of what you do well
or what you can start to do
from today…

May the Lord be generous
in increasing your love
and make you love one another *(1 Th 3:12)*.

Middle age

When we do get to be middle-aged,
if we are not already there,
will we realize that we must
    find time,
    make time,
we, who have so little time,
    who are so caught up in work,
    who are so busy living?
Yes, will we realize
that we must take time,
our precious time,
to turn inward,
search through our souls,
look inside?
We must lose time,
    to reflect,
    to meditate,
    to pray!
If we are always in a hurry,
if we never have any time,
if we are always moving on
to some job or another,
can we ever become truly wise?
Our lives will be as erratic
as a boat without a rudder.
We shall be tossed around
like a leaf in the wind.

To become mature,
we have
    to take time,

        to look at a flower,
        to smile at the laugh of a child,
        to be enraptured by sunset.

We have to stop saying:
"I have no time to waste".
We must, above all, turn inward,
become pilgrims to the core of our hearts.

Since,
in time,
in the deepest part of ourselves,
we shall find
        wonderful treasures,
        unknown worlds,
        unexplored shores.
We shall be astonished at all that is within us.

We shall enjoy these inward paths,
and our delight shall come
from these moments of fulfillment.
We shall see
how the silent dialogue with ourselves
will give new value to life.

And if our dialogue brings us to listen,
not only to ourselves,
but to Him Who is closer to us
than our very selves,
to meet Him Who has chosen us
before we ever existed,
then our lives will not be a sequence of "doings",
but will become a burst of "being",
and we shall reach perfect maturity
which is "in the measure of Christ in the fullness"
                                    (Ep 4:13).

— "People who take themselves seriously,
  are they the wisest?"
— "No", said the wise man.
— "So, who is wise?"
  "Children,
  or the old who are growing old well.
  Those who know
  that the earth can turn quite easily
  without them.
  Those who are overjoyed
  with a dewdrop or a rose.
Those for whom the Most High is important.
People like these are wise",
said the wise man.

An idea

Before going beyond an idea,
you must at least catch up with it…!

(Words of a wise old man).

Dying successfully!

Lord,
I am going to die.
The twenty-fourth hour will strike soon!
It is December in my life!
I know my days are counted,
the doctor has told me.
The thread of my life is snatched from me!

It's hard,
I love life.
My head is full of plans,
but now, what good is that?
The only plan that matters
is how to succeed in dying.
Really,
the only important thing in life
is to succeed in one's death!

When I look back on my life,
I can see clearly that it wasn't all good:
there were failures,
bad patches,
and worse still:
     hate,
     bitterness,
     ambitions,
     selfishness,
     sins...
I spoiled lots of chances to love You.
But I know that Your goodness and mercy
have forgotten and forgiven all that.

And there were a few good things:
    service done,
    forgiveness given,
    prayer.
Your love and mercy have taken them into Your heart!

For the time I have left to live,
Lord,
    let me give myself to Your will,
    let me fit myself to Your mysterious desires,
    let me put my hand in Your hand.
I give myself to You in everything.
Put Your hand on my shoulder,
guide my feet in Your path.
Show me the way, Your way!
In Your goodness,
welcome me into Paradise,
where I may see You face to face,
and live with You
and with those I love
who are already with You
in an endless happiness.

Amen.

We have never failed to pray for you
and what we ask God
is that through perfect wisdom
and spiritual understanding
you should reach the fullest knowledge of his will
(Col 1:9).

V
PEOPLE

The listener

She is a very ordinary woman.
Her only diploma was
her sixth grade card
and her highest certificate was
that of her Holy Communion.
She raised her family,
six children,
    peacefully,
    gently,
    humbly.
Today,
they are married
with children of their own,
''Doing well'', as she says.
She lives alone
in her big house.
Her husband died three years ago.
Yet, she is never alone.
Her phone never stops.
She doesn't phone,
she would hate to ''bother'' anyone.
But everyone calls her,
    her children,
    the sons-in-law,
    the daughters-in-law,
    the grandchildren.
To talk of important things
or nothing at all.
And she listens
patiently
for hours.

And then, they visit her;
they tell her about themselves,
they ask advice...
She listens
>to everything,
>to all,
>all the time.

Everyone finds her interesting...

But it is perhaps
because she is interested in them.
She has learned so much:
>good things and bad things,
>whims and unhappiness,
>deep secrets...

Everyone believes in her,
yet she says little...
She rarely gives advice.
She listens... and that's it,
without ever tiring.
And while the other speaks,
he finds in
>her attention,
>her kindness,
>her love,
the answer to his questions,
the solution to his problems.

And, at the end of the day,
before she sleeps,
she sits in her rocking chair,
thinking about those she has listened to
during the day.

She says her rosary
in front of a statue of Our Lady.
This is where she draws
      her strength,
      her depth of attention,
      her deep love for others.

It is
      in her prayer,
      in her simple faith,
that her love is renewed
      constantly,
      wonderfully.

Oh God, I know that You listen
each time I pray:
You are the great listener!
Let me remember to pray...
to give You the chance to listen to me...
Oh God, on our way in life,
let us meet people who listen.
It is so precious,
it is so rare!
And, if You will,
let us be in our turn,
listeners for those who need it!

Amen.

Robert

Robert had a corn on his toe,
it bothered him quite a bit:
he limped awkwardly
and never missed a chance
to complain about it.
In fact, his corn was "on his mind"
and he was busy
putting it
into everybody else's mind!

Robert had to visit an old aunt
who was in a home
for the chronically sick.
She shared her room
with a woman of thirty-eight
who had multiple sclerosis,
four children
and would be in bed
for the rest of her life.

She was always cheerful
and never complained.
Robert had to swallow a lump in his throat.

From that day,
Robert stopped complaining
and boring everyone
with his "bump".
He limped less and less
and thanked God every day
for his good health!

In all things give thanks to God *(1 Th 5:18)*.

I complained that I had no shoes
until the day I met someone
who had no feet *(Chinese proverb)*.

The children

There are three of them.
They come regularly
to play in my garden.
When I am there,
I am the umpire in their games.
They are all about five years old...
just little devils... cute!

There is also Shirley,
she is six.
When I come home from work,
she meets me
and brings me a flower
that she puts in a jar
on the kitchen table.
Of course, she has to have a flower
from my flower-beds.
She asks if I have had a good day.
Am I very tired?
Would I play with her?
Wonderful little Shirley!

I must not forget Jimmy.
A little imp of three.
He follows me like my shadow.
He is at the 'why' stage.
Why do you do this?... or that?
Why did you come home late today?
I was waiting for you, did you know?
Dear little Jimmy...

Children...
They are like clear crystal,
    transparent,
    bright,
    genuine.
They are dew in the morning,
coolness in the evening!
They are
    the smile of God,
    the poem in the heart,
    the pearl in the hand!

They are
    reconciliation,
    love,
    life.

They are
    complete trust,
    generous love,
    lively simplicity.
They are what we are no longer.
They are our teachers!
Do we know how to listen to them?
Jesus knew that,
Who loved them so much!

God, why...?

David is a brilliant surgeon:
he took all the prizes at the university
and, in the hospital, he is loved
by all the patients;
the nurses like to be with him
when he operates.
His office is never empty,
full of crowds
of waiting, trustful patients.
His reputation is genuine:
his competence is only equalled by his care
and his warmth is as strong
as his devotion to duty.
He is one of the rare specialists in town
who still makes housecalls.

David has just got back
from visiting a patient.
He has braved the snowstorm,
the gusts of wind,
the Arctic cold.
Suddenly his car stops,
he can neither go back nor forward:
he is caught in a snowbank.
He opens the trunk,
take out a snowshovel
and feverishly,
in the biting wind,
he shovels away the snow.
He can't free his car.
How the devil did he drive in there?

He lifts shovelful after shovelful.
He is sweating,
hot despite the cold.
He is panting now.
Suddenly he feels a pain
like a whip across his chest...
He sits down on the seat
to catch his breath.
He breathes more and more painfully.
He sighs,
he gasps.
Eight minutes later he is dead!
The next day he is found,
frozen,
under the snow.

David is dead forty-two years old.
He had a wife,
three children, a shining career,
a tremendous sense of duty!

* * *

Ian has just finished his law studies:
his professors had praised his intelligence.
He has already been hired
by one of the most distinguished law firms in the city.
A glowing future stretches in front of him.
Tucking his diploma under his arm,
he jumps cheerfully on his bike,
to see Carol,
his fiancée,
happy to be together,
to make plans for their future home.
He rides easily,

happily,
his head in the clouds.
His heart is rejoicing,
sunshine is everywhere.
Life is just wonderful,
he tells himself cheerfully.

But just then
the front wheel of his bike gets caught
in the groove of a tramway car.
He can't control his bike,
loses his balance,
falls on the concrete roadway.
Ian never gets up.
What was happened?
Passersby rush over.
There is a pool of blood under his head.
Quick! An ambulance!
At the hospital all that the doctors can say is
that it is all over.

A broken career,
a life snuffed out in its prime.
So much knowledge lost,
love broken for always.

There are thousands of stories
like these in the world.
We never get used to such things.
We always say: "It's not possible"
and then:
"Why, O Lord?"
Why is life so hard?
Why does death cut down some really good lives?
Why does suffering come
to the hearts of those

who love each other?
Why? Why? Why?
It's crazy,
there's no sense in it,
it's foolish.
Why, Lord, why?

Oh, God,
I do not ask
that You explain
the mystery of death.
I do not believe You create these evil things.
You cannot want evil.
But,
I ask You
Who have conquered death,
Who are Life,
to give Your Life to those who have lost it,
to give it to them for ever,
     in fullness,
     in beauty,
     in good fortune.
I pray to You
     for those still here,
     for the family of David,
     for Carol.
Have pity on them
in their sadness.
Be their consolation,
in a hope
which can withstand all troubles,
so that they may be certain
that some day
they will again be reunited
and they will never, never be separated.
May Your untiring, everlasting Love,

surround us all
for ever!

He will destroy death for ever.
The Lord Yahweh will wipe away
the tears from every cheek.
For Yahweh has said so *(Is 25:8).*

An allergy

Little Jenny has an allergy
which makes her grumble and complain!
She found about it
one Easter
when she was given a big chocolate rabbit.
Can you imagine anything sadder
than a little girl
who is allergic to chocolate?
Especially at Easter?

Well, there are worse things
in life
than an allergy to chocolate.
It may be good
but we can get along
without it in our lives.

But, to be allergic,
to bread, milk, vegetables...
now that would be serious!
And if we were allergic to Jesus... well!!!

Cut off from me, you can do nothing *(Jn 15:5)*.

Anyone who does eat My flesh
and drink My blood
has eternal life *(Jn 6:54)*.

I am too busy...

Doug was in the hospital
and would have liked me to visit him.
But, in the end, I didn't make it;
not because I didn't want to,
but there just wasn't enough time.
I am too busy,
always in a hurry.
There are too many meetings!
Doug understood
but I was sad and so was he!

Mary had a party
for her little daughter's birthday.
She invited me, but I couldn't go.
I had an appointment.
Mary and her daughter were sad
and so was I.
The wind of efficiency carries me on.
I am too busy.
Perhaps I should rethink my priorities.

George phoned me the other evening:
a real emergency!
His son was threatening to commit suicide.
I had to cancel a meeting to go to see him.
I am so busy
that it seems I have no time
for people who need me,
and whom I need too!

There is something
not running properly in my life.
I am forgetting the main point.
Efficiency can cut down freedom,
work can reduce the attention
we give to others.

How did I reach this point?
How could I let myself be taken over
like this?
I've lost all free time.

You'll have to unburden yourself, old man!
You must take on less,
break away from these scheduled meetings.
You must make time,
find time for others.

There was one of the Pharisees called Nicodemus,
a leading Jew, who came to Jesus *by night* (Jn 3:1-2).

Fred

Drinking...
Drinking, that is Fred's weakness.

In the beginning
he'd just have a glass with friends:
    office parties,
    business meeting,
    social evenings...
Then it all became an excuse for drink:
he worked harder than most,
he needed a stimulant...
He had a problem, a worry,
He took a "pick me up"...
he had a success,
he had to celebrate!
His wife pointed out one day
that he "took something" every evening.
"Don't worry", he said to her.

Fred had to face the evidence:
he could not do without a drink.
So, he decided to give it up.
He had seen some friends manage that pretty well.
Of his own free will,
he gave up the evenings out
but many times,
it was stronger than he was.
He joined the AA.
He said with enthusiasm that he has progressed!
But, at last,
seeing that nothing was really ended,

he stopped going to the local bar.
He goes there now and again
but he knows himself.

"I shall die an alcoholic"
he said to me the other day.
"I shall spend my life trying to win,
probably there will be good intervals,
but I shall always fall back again".

"Trying to win"...
How many of us are doing just that
all our lives,
never succeeding completely!
How many, damaged by life, will suffer always?
Wounds, known or unknown to others!
Alcohol, drugs, homosexuality,
dissolute living, robbery, etc.

Psychologists talk in truth of sickness, mania, etc.
Spiritual people talk of trials sent by God,
"sting in the flesh" *(2 Cor 12:7)*.
Moralists talk of "sin"...

Whatever the specialists say,
whatever the wounds are,
those wounded by life will always need to find
the hope which helps them to live
in the midst of their trials.

And if they are believers,
it is in the heart of their faith
that they can find hope.
It is much more than a hope
that conditions will improve...
It is a belief that one day

God, in his mercy and goodness,
will establish everything
     in beauty,
     in uprightness,
     in completeness.

Lord, give Fred and his family
the courage to accept their state,
give him the strength
to keep trying to win,
even if he doesn't always manage it.
Let him realize
that You love him deeply as he is,
     with his good qualities,
     with his failings,
     with his weakness,
     with his struggles,
that You have put Your hand on his shoulder,
that his name is written in Your heart,
and Your love is greater than his difficulties.
Let him find out
that what really matters
is not the success,
but that he never stops trying!

Let him know
with absolute certainty,
that he, just as he is,
is set for holiness.
And that above all
he finds in the faith
that You gave him at baptism,
in the faith of his family,
Your hope,
this small hope,
yet great,

and strong,
and powerful.
So, with his hand in Your hand,
he will accept to live,
wounded by alcohol,
but also wounded by Your love
which will never let him go.

Amen.

I will restore you to your former state *(Ezk 16:55)*.

The Lord Jesus Christ will transfigure
these wretched bodies of ours
into copies of His glorious body *(Ph 3:21)*.

I will betroth you to myself for ever,
I will betroth you with integrity and justice,
with tenderness and love,
I will betroth you to myself with faithfulness,
and you will come to know Yahweh *(Ho 2:22)*.

Harry...

Harry had worked all his life:
Monday to Friday
from seven in the morning to six at night.
He had been the maintenance man
in a textile factory.
He had worked at some small job all his life.
The newspaper had never printed his photograph,
the radio had never spoken of him,
the television never showed him in the little screen.

Once at the factory,
they gave him a party.
He had worked there for twenty-five years.
The boss gave a little talk
and gave him a medal-souvenir.
Harry cried a little.
But the next day, he was back at work
as if nothing has happened...

By careful budgeting,
Harry had put aside a little money
for his retirement.
Nothing much!
He couldn't go to Europe, or even Florida.
But he and his wife would be able
to live carefully.
He loved his wife, Gerrie,
a woman so courageous and so loving,
his eight children
and eleven grandchildren.
They were his real fortune,

his great pride,
his family,
his wonderful family!

It's nine months now
since Harry retired.
In the beginning, it was good.
Harry enjoyed the affection of his family
and took time to enjoy life.
Then after three months
he began having headaches,
continual headaches.
He didn't say anything at first,
hoping not to worry anyone
and that it would go away.
But it didn't go.
He, who had never been sick,
found he had to go to the doctor.
Examinations, laboratory tests…
they found nothing!

He went home,
reassured with good medical advice
and fortified with pills.
He managed to hang on
for two more months:
thin,
crabby,
glum,
stay at home.
Then his wife said they must go to the city
to see a specialist.
Brain X-ray and encephalogram:
Harry had a tumor.
They tried to operate
but it was too late.

Harry is finished,
just waiting for the end.
His wife, his children, his friends wonder:
"Why? Is this fair?
Harry didn't deserve this".

Before such basic questions,
     such radical situations,
where do we find an answer?
where do we find comfort and hope?

The path of life,
is it a dead end?
a no-through way?
Or is there a way out for Harry
and his family?

Slowly,
painfully
but with determination,
they are on a new path:
it is impossible
that there is nothing
after.
There must be
something:
light after darkness,
joy after sadness,
union after separation.
And hope, despite everything, is born
in Harry's heart
and his family.
A hope which goes beyond pain
and suffering
and death.
A hope which changes

little by little
to an expectation,
which leans on Him
who said:
''I am the Life''.

I am the Resurrection and the Life.
If anyone believes in Me,
even though he dies,
he will live.
And whoever lives and believes in me
will never die *(Jn 11:25-26).*

We want you to be quite certain, brothers,
about those who have died,
to make sure that you do not grieve about them,
like the other people who have no hope *(1 Th 4:13).*

Always have your answer ready for people
who ask you the reason
for your hope that you all have *(1 P 3:15).*

Little Sebastian...

Little Sebastian
was running after his dog, Fido,
gamboling here and there.

Fido crossed the street
and, in turn, trampled some pansies,
crushed some carnations,
broke some nasturtiums.

The neighbor, who loved her flowers,
told her husband about the happening
of the day.

The husband, who sincerely loved his wife,
scolded Sebastian, who once again,
had crossed the street
to fetch his ball.

Little Sebastian
frightened by the man's voice
began to cry.
He went home broken-hearted.

Sebastian's father, who loved his son,
crossed the street
and told off the neighbor's husband.
It was a great "telling off".

Each one defended his love:
  the father, his Sebastian!
  the husband, his wife!

the wife, her flowers!
    Sebastian, his dog!
Finally, they had enough common sense
to see how ridiculous the situation was.

Friendship between neighbors,
love for a child
are worth more than a few flowers.

You should agree among yourselves
    and be sympathetic.
Love the brothers, have compassion and be humble.
Never pay back one wrong with another,
or an angry word with another one;
instead, pay back with a blessing.
That is what you are called to do,
 so that you inherit a blessing yourself *(1 P 3:8-9)*.

Beatrice

She always talks loudly.
You would think she is always angry.
It's as if we were all deaf...
She drowns us all.
It's just her way.
She doesn't know
    the charm of soft words,
    the pleasure in subtlety,
    the richness in silence.
She deafens us with her thunder.
She wears us out,
she is exasperating...

But... she has a heart of gold.
She would give her shirt to help someone.
She doesn't count her time or her money
to do a good turn.
All that is hers
belongs to everyone.
When she lends,
it's as good as given away,
since she never checks up.
That's her way!

Lord, human nature
is a small mystery.
We can never finish
trying to grasp
what it is.

There are those we like
and those we don't,
those we please
and those we displease.

Lord, may I recognize you in everyone,
     in the generosity of some,
     in the knowledge of others,
     in the gentleness of this one,
     in the strength of that one,
     in the grumpiness of the first,
     in the thunder of the second.

May I shut my eyes and my mouth
at what sets my teeth on edge,
knowing
that there must be things
in me
which irritate others.

Amen.

For You, O God, even silence is praise *(Ps 65:2)*.

Frank

It is 8.15 and Frank is driving to work.
The radio is playing a Mozart concerto,
pleasing both his ear and his heart.
The countryside fills his eyes:
    rolling oats,
    grazing cows...
and his nose picks up the subtle, bitter smells:
    freshly cut clover,
    buckwheat,
    manure...

Frank is floating lightly, joyfully...
He feels like
    birdsong in his heart,
    butterflies in his eyes,
    music in his fingers...
he is feeling rapture in his soul!

Today he could take on
all his problems,
enough energy to do all the jobs,
enthusiasm to spare for everyone.
He is ready to do his bit in "building the world",
as he has heard it said somewhere.
What wonderful weather,
what a great day it will be!
He is in seventh heaven!

But slowly,
hardly noticing it,
Frank has left the countryside
and has reached the bridge leading to the city.

Traffic jam!
His car is caught in a bottle neck.
On the right,
the sound of the engine of a large truck
has killed off Mozart, a long time ago.
On the left,
the exhaust pipe of a limousine
has swallowed the smell
of clover and buckwheat, even manure.
Frank can no longer see
     green fields,
     white daisies,
     peaceful herds.
In front of him, behind him,
steel,
concrete,
noise,
to make you lose your hearing!
Carbon dioxide,
to make you lose your sense of smell!
Frank is
     crushed,
     poisoned,
     in a nightmare.
He rolls up the car windows
but it is a waste of time:
he is suffocating.
His car moves forward,
inch by inch.
Its engine heats up.
So does he.
God!
Hell could be no worse.
Cursed pollution!

He gets off the bridge at 9.30.
He arrives at the office,
    breathless,
    impatient,
    exhausted.

That's the way it is in life!
    Sunny days,
    cloudy days...
    Moonlit nights,
    nights as black as ink...
    Joy,
    sadness...
    Enthusiasm,
    disgust...
Take heart, Frank!
Sometimes the sky is blue,
sometimes grey.
But the real sky is in your heart,
and it's up to you
and you alone,
that it stays blue,
despite pollution!

It's true,
we create our own good luck
or bad luck!

Dick and Paddy

Dick is a grouch!
He is always crotchety.
He looks cross
and doesn't smile much.
Ask him to do something… he'll grumble.
But he'll always do it!

Paddy is good-natured:
he smiles easily
and with a lot of charm.
He is pleasant company.
Ask him to do anything
and he's glad to agree
but more often than not,
he doesn't do it!

I wish Dick could have Paddy's smile
and Paddy be as dependable as Dick.
But, all things considered,
I think I prefer crotchety Dick
to undependable Paddy…
What about you?

A man had two sons.
He went and said to the first:
''My boy, you go and work in the vineyard today''.
He answered: ''I will not go''.
But afterwards thought better of it and went.

The man then went and said the same thing
to the second who answered: ''Certainly, sir''.
But he did not go.
Which of the two did the father's will? *(Mt 21:28-31).*

The old man

He didn't talk much now,
not that he was mute,
but he preferred to listen
and much more to watch.

Six years ago he retired,
or rather he had to retire
since he was sixty-five.

At first, he found plenty to do,
looking after the lawn,
fixing up the house, odd jobs...
Then, little by little,
he seemed at a loose end,
bored, weary of days,
that never seemed to end...

In a year he aged terribly:
    white hair,
    rheumatism,
    high blood pressure,
    heart problems...
He was dying
from nothing to do,
of not knowing what to do!
All day long,
sitting in his rocking chair,
his pipe in his mouth,
silently he watched his wife,
still active and working,
busy over household chores.

He thought,
he reflected,
he meditated.
Sunday,
his children,
and especially his grandchildren,
came and visited him.
Then, he woke up again!
> never tired of listening to them,
> looking at them,
> contemplating them.

As if silently, he could give them
something of himself, his life;
as if he wanted to mark in his memory,
> the blond hair of Lisa,
> Mark's blue eyes,
> the happy chatter of baby Katie;

as if he saw himself in his children,
when he was their age,
> as strong as Paul,
> as full of initiative as John,
> as happy as Peter.

To grow old,
> in beauty,
> and in wisdom,

it's an art,
a challenge.
You can't do it alone.
The song puts it well:
''When you get old,
you need your children
to help you finish the road''.

The elderly call us,
they teach us too.

If they listen to us,
we must listen to them.
If they look at us,
we must really look at them too,
because some day, we shall be in their place!

The crown of the aged is their children *(Pr 17:6).*

Do not despise your mother in her old age *(Pr 23:22).*

Kathleen

Kathleen is alone.
She has been a widow for four months.
Left alone with three children.
Three very young children.
She has found work...
You have to earn a living!
You have to earn something
for yourself and the children.
But you have to pay the baby-sitter, too.
The end of the month is terrible:
rent, telephone, electricity
and medicine if you are sick
and the odd treats
that children must have,
now and again.

Kathleen must add it all up,
down to the last penny.
Income, wage, family allowance...
payments too!
If it all works out,
if nothing unforeseen happens,
she can make both ends meet.
But, if anything happens,
it's a nightmare.
Are there many months
when everything goes as planned?
More often than not,
Kathleen is at the end of her tether.
Sometimes despair knocks on her door,
depression too.

The children are sad
and it's sad to see sad children!

Oh God,
Who looked tenderly
    at the children,
    at the widow of Naim,
    at the poor and the weak,
arouse in the heart of the rich
enough generosity and kindness
to help Kathleen and her children.
Put Your hand on her,
so that she may find You
through the one who will help her.

Amen.

Never turn your face from any poor man,
and God will never turn His from you *(Tb 4:7).*

Pure, unspoiled religion,
in the eyes of God our Father, is this:
looking after orphans and widows,
in their distress... *(Jm 1:27).*

Just a monk

He had the head of a patriarch
and the smile of a child.
His look was as clear as crystal
and his hands the shape of welcome.
He spoke very little
but everyone went,
just to listen to him.
He had nothing,
but he gave to everyone.
He had no degree,
yet knew everything.
He was at once:
     presence,
     joy,
     tenderness,
     peace,
     security
     and love.

They came from all over to see him.
He gave something which made everyone feel better.
It was as if he gilded us a little
with the golden quality of his sunshine.
And each went away better
for having met him.

He was not one of the great ones of this world,
he had
     no money,

no power,
no knowledge,
nothing.
Just a monk!
He spent his time in prayer,
fasting
and working in the fields.

Little by little,
he had got rid of the things
that weigh down most of us:
    pride,
    anger,
    jealousy,
    covetousness,
    greed,
    ambition…
And he was filled only with God.

He had become free and liberating.
He had become peaceful and pacifying.
The meeting with his God
    had enraptured him like Elijah at Horeb,
    dazzled him like Moses on Sinai,
    transfigured him like Jesus on Tabor.
Poor in everything
but rich with God and God alone,
when he met people
it was God he gave them.
That is why people always came back
to see him!

Oh God, give us men and women of this pattern.
Even if we are not able to be like them,
do You know how much good it does us
to meet them now and again?

... And the sons of Israel would see
the face of Moses radiant *(Ex 34:35).*

There in their presence He was transfigured,
His face shone like the sun
and His clothes became as white as the light *(Mt 17:2).*

William

William is a magnificent specimen of humanity:
    athlete's physique,
    well set up,
    solid body,
    pleasant face,
    flashing smile.
His talk is interesting, he is well read.
His personality flutters the hearts of the ladies...!

But William is not just charming, he is also brilliant.
At college, he made a clean sweep of the prizes;
at the university, he was the dream student
of the most demanding professors.
Now he has a job in a big company:
    fantastic salary,
    steady promotion,
    all the fringe benefits...

In fact, William is a man
overflowing with the good things in life:
    health,
    intelligence,
    good job,
    social prestige,
    well thought of family,
    money,
    property,
    etc.
William is a living strength,
    a solid rock,
    a great success.

He has hardly any time to pray,
just too busy living!
He only trusts himself!

That's where his power lies!
William's God is very far away
which never bothers him.
The real gods for William are
        his intelligence,
        his contacts,
        his vitality,
        his reputation,
        his creativity,
        his money...
Thinking it over,
William adores himself
and only in himself does he put his faith.

And yet,
one of these days,
his strength will grow less,
others will take his place,
his health will fail.
What will become of the great William
if God has no place
        in his actions,
        in his success?

Do not store up treasure
        for yourselves on earth,
where moths and woodworms
        destroy them
and thieves
        can break in and steal.
But store up treasure
        in heaven... *(Mt 6:19-20).*

What then will a man gain
if he wins the whole world
and ruins his life? *(Mt 16:26).*

But when the Son of Man comes,
will He find any faith on the earth? *(Lk 18:8).*

The old lady

She came to the sea,
to breathe its salty air,
to contemplate the ocean.
She came alone,
at seventy five!
Outside it was 30° C.
The children and their parents left the motel
in swimsuits.
She went out
    a handkerchief on her head,
    silk gloves on her hands,
    gabardine on her back!
The adults looked at her
out of the corner of their eyes;
the young laughed among themselves
and the children giggled...
With her bright eyes,
she saw all that
and understood.

She sat on a bench on the boardwalk,
facing the sea
for hours and hours on end.
There, she watched the children
building sandcastles on the beach.
The young playing in the water...
She listened
    to the rolling waves,
    to the wind on the sand.
Then she took a small book,
a prayer book
from her bag.

And quietly,
bothering no one,
in front of the vastness of the sea,
she said the prayers of her childhood.
Other times,
she took her rosary
from her bag
and hid it in the folds of her coat.
For two weeks,
every day,
she did the same thing.
Alone!
Then one morning,
a taxi came for her.
Who could explain the mystery
hidden in this old lady?
No one knows.
Was it a fight against death?
Living her youth again?
Preparation to go?
Should we laugh or cry?
We shall never know.

Old people have things to teach us.
If only we knew how to listen to them,
see them,
contemplate them!
If we know how to love them,
enjoy them
and serve them!
If we know how to understand!

Mark and Mary

The mother had made a delicious cake:
banana and almond.
I don't understand recipes,
but the cooks said it was magnificent.
Anyway,
tasting it,
I found it superb.
Little Mark,
aged five years old,
asked his mother for a slice.
He tested it with the tip of his tongue,
spat it out
and said to his mother:
"Your cake is horrible,
I don't want any".
A childish reaction certainly,
but the mother still loves Mark
in spite of his refusal.
She made other cakes.
For a mother is made that way:
she doesn't shut up her heart,
she goes on loving.

The father saw a bicycle in the store window,
just the right size for Mary,
his little six year old.
It was a long time
she had been wanting one like this!
So thinking of his love for his daughter,
the father went into the store
and bought the bicycle.

Mary is thrilled,
hugs her father
for this wonderful present.

Two days later,
coming home from work
the father finds Mary in angry tears.
''The bike you gave me is no good!
It's broken already!
Keep your present''.
The father, patiently,
takes the bicycle into his shed
and repairs it.
Then he gives it back to Mary
who is happy again.
Fathers are made to forgive
and to love.
This is where we learn about life
and the fathers and mothers who love
do so spontaneously.

God is our Father
and we are His children.
In our forgetfulness and lack of gratitude,
He reacts with love
just like human mothers and fathers.

What father among you would hand his son a stone
when he asked for bread?
Or hand him a snake instead of a fish?
Or hand him a scorpion if he asked for an egg?
If you, who are evil, know
how to give your children what is good,
how much more will the heavenly Father
give the Holy Spirit to those who ask him? *(Lk 11:11-13)*.

"Know-it-all" Joe

He judged everything,
looking down from
his vast knowledge.
He had his say on everything
from the vantage point of his ideas.
He questioned nothing,
especially not himself.
Anyway, why wonder?
        He had read "everything",
        he thought of "everything",
        he weighed "everything".
He had
        found out everything,
        discovered everything...
        Everything, absolutely everything!

And if, by chance, someone mentioned an idea
he hadn't thought of,
he had a ready reaction:
"That's old fashioned,
you're dreaming in technicolor,
that's just a utopian idea".
How could it be otherwise?
He was a little astonished,
a little put out,
that people did not come back for his advice,
were not more interested in his ideas,
left him alone more and more.
It was about the only thing he couldn't explain.

"Why do people leave an empty space around me?"
he said.
Really, it wasn't other people who made it empty,
he did it himself,
the poor guy who thought himself so rich.
He who doesn't know
when to give up,
abandon his opinions,
will keep them sterile within himself!
There is only one way to create
even ideas:
you have to give up something of yourself,
humbly.
Then, little by little,
you see them born in others,
often improved too!
And that is wonderful!

What do you have that was not given to you?
And if it was given,
how can you boast as though it were not? *(1 Cor 4:7).*

Imprimerie des Éditions Paulines
250, boul. St-François nord
Sherbrooke, Qc, J1E 2B9

Imprimé au Canada — Printed in Canada